WHAT IS
LOVE?

ALSO BY TARO GOLD

Open Your Mind, Open Your Life
A Book of Eastern Wisdom
(Large Second Volume)

Open Your Mind, Open Your Life
A Little Book of Eastern Wisdom
(Miniature First Volume)

The Tao of Mom
The Wisdom of Mothers from East to West

Please visit www.TaroGold.com to learn more
about the author and his work.

WHAT IS
LOVE?

*A Simple Buddhist Guide to
Romantic Happiness*

TARO GOLD

**Andrews McMeel
Publishing**

Kansas City

ISBN: 0-7407-3838-0

Library of Congress Control Number: 2003100786

03 04 05 06 07 TWP 10 9 8 7 6 5 4 3 2 1

Book design by Holly Camerlinck
Illustrations by Matthew Taylor

With affection and gratitude
to my parents, David and Carol,
for showing me
through their love for each other
an enlightened example
of romantic happiness

Contents

ACKNOWLEDGMENTS

A small book like this appears deceptively easy to create yet actually requires the devotion of many talented people. I owe loving appreciation to the women and men behind the scenes of this and all my books, especially: Sheree Bykofsky, my friend and consummate literary agent, and her unflagging and witty associate, Janet Rosen, for believing from the outset in a greater vision; Jennifer Fox, my talented and insightful editor, and her all-star team at Andrews McMeel, for nurturing each of my ideas to fruition; Dr. Daisaku Ikeda, for sharing with me over the years his vast knowledge of Buddhism; Laurie Viera Rigler, for her literary guidance, without which I would surely be lost; Lisa Carter Kirk, for weaving sheer grace into my work; and all the loves of my life, for helping me develop the greatest of fortunes—the treasures of the heart.

AUTHOR'S NOTE

The most important thing I can say to you is this: You, just as you are, deserve all the love and joy in the world.

The second most important thing I can say to you is this: You are already capable of attracting such love and joy to you. You may not feel that way now, but read on. There is a light at the end of the tunnel, and it's closer than you think.

Simple, practical answers to love's fundamental questions fill this book, which is based on the universal principles of Buddhism. By leading us first to become happy within, Buddhist teachings offer powerful, effective guidance on finding and maintaining the romantic happiness of our dreams.

Buddhism is a way of thinking, a way of being, more than a way of believing. Established some 2,500 years ago by a passionate young prince named Shakyamuni (also known as Gautama Buddha or Siddhartha), Buddhism is the practice of living a joyful life. Its intent is to help all people attain absolute happiness, regardless of any distinctions such as gender, race, religion, or sexuality. Simply put, Buddhism highlights the ultimate joy and wisdom inherent in us all. It shows us that we already have what we need to live "happily ever after" by encouraging us to free our hearts and minds from prejudice and delusion, tap into the shining essence at the center of our being, and seize control of our destiny through positive actions.

With this slim volume, I endeavor to explore the issue of happiness in love from the essential Buddhist view, free from cultural bias. The result, I hope, is a treasury of advice that readers from every background will find inspirational, thought provoking, and romantically enlightening.

*M*ore valuable than treasures in a storehouse
are treasures of the body, and the treasures of the heart
are the most valuable of all.

— NICHIREN

❧

*Y*ou may search the universe for someone
more worthy of your love and affection
than you are yourself, but such a person does not exist.

— BUDDHIST PROVERB

❧

*J*ust as a song is a partnership of music and lyrics,
partners in love are equal individuals who,
at the same time, perform a melody of life together.

— DAISAKU IKEDA

LOVE AND ILLUSION

The Outer Path:

SEARCHING THROUGH THE FANTASY

Love—

n. a powerful emotion manifesting in
deep affection, devotion, or sexual desire.

(Webster's New Dictionary and Thesaurus)

*W*hat is love? That is the great, eternal question. Our world today is flooded with images of love in songs, films, advertising, and television that always seem to end in an effortless happily-ever-after. It's a beautiful, romantic, and dreamy picture of love that our popular culture has painted for us. Inundated by unrealistic fantasies, who could blame us for expecting that love would be the answer to all of our dreams, and that when we fall in love our ecstatic emotions would last forever?

Around the globe and across the ages, philosophers and poets have been considered experts on the subject and have written more about love than anyone else, yet they repeatedly contradict one another in hopelessly irreconcilable terms. Some call love "a sickness full of woes" and "a mighty pain," while others assure us that love is a "many-splendored thing" and "the sweetest delight on Earth."

Falling in love can certainly be a tremendous joy. From the

Buddhist view, however, the blissful expectations and intense feelings of rapture we associate with love are not true love but the symptoms of love—mere illusions. And, as with all illusions, they can vanish as quickly as they appear.

Our collective love affair with illusion plays itself out in the reality that 60 percent of marriages collapse, regardless of the dramatic and oft-spoken vow "till death do us part." Include the number of other long-term relationships that fail, such as common law and gay partnerships, and it's enough to make us wonder what has happened, or hasn't happened, to create such a puzzling state of affairs in this thing called love.

*L*ove with patience, gentleness, and truth
gives birth to enlightenment.

— BUDDHIST PROVERB

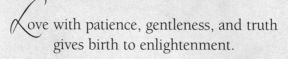

*T*he magic of first love is our ignorance that it could ever end.

— ISAAC D'ISRAELI

*W*hen two love each other, the very angels leave heaven to
visit their home and sing for joy.

— BRAHMAN PROVERB

*T*he rose is the flower of love because of its painfully sharp
thorns, concealed beneath the beauty of its fragrant blossoms.

— VALERIUS MAXIMUS

Perhaps our conundrums in love have something to do with the fact that we are not taught about love the way we are taught about other important facts of life. In school, everyone gets math, history, and language classes, but how many of us get a class in love? (Sex education doesn't count. Learning about sex and learning about love are entirely different matters.)

Why is it that something we regard with such value and importance as love receives less instruction than the average driver's education class? Is there nothing we can learn about love except by experience? We don't normally learn to drive a car by crashing until we get it right, but this seems to be the strategy of many people learning the ways of love. Perhaps we expect that since love is a natural sort of drive, it is supposed to work itself out magically. That's like expecting to drive a car with your eyes closed. It may work for a little while, but it will soon come to an abrupt ending.

Still, if you're like most people, you'd probably say that love is simple—it's finding "the right one" to love that's difficult. Although it's true that finding an ideal love partner can be challenging, the reality is that it's even more challenging to sustain the love you create once you find the right person. Falling in love and making a commitment, even with "the right one," isn't the end—it's the beginning. Maybe because feelings of love come so naturally to us, we are ever more shocked to find that loving relationships require a great deal of effort.

So what causes the great number of breakups in love? Is it that we are unprepared to do the work love requires, or is it something else? Depending on whom you ask, you might hear any number of explanations, including media influence, genetic predisposition, or a shift in modern family values. To some extent, I'm sure every reason we can think of for the breakdowns in our own relationships probably holds some truth, especially when we talk about our partners. "He or she didn't communicate, was immature, emotionally unavailable, afraid of commitment, untrustworthy"—you can fill in the blank yourself. According to Buddhism, however, the most fundamental source of difficulties in love is found not in our mates but in our own desires and behaviors—within our own thoughts, words, and deeds. (That is, our karma, which we'll discuss in more detail later on.)

Yep, that's right. Your actions, your thoughts, not those of your partner, are what determine your success in love as well as in all other areas of your life. This knowledge is powerfully freeing, for no longer are you reliant on others for your happiness. You alone direct the course of your love and life and attract happiness on your own terms.

*T*o fall in love is easy, but it is a hard quest worth making
to find a comrade through whose steady presence
one becomes the person one desires to be.

—ANNA LOUISE STRONG

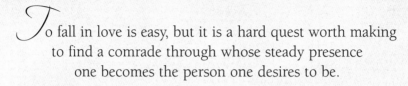

*I*gnorance with love is better than knowledge without it.

—BUDDHIST PROVERB

*L*ove is often the exchange of two illusions.

—CHAMFORT

*T*o love is to desire something one lacks.

—PLATO

On my twenty-fifth birthday, I lamented to my great-grandmother that I feared I would never meet "the right one" for me. The following week, she sent me a heartening letter in which she recounted the story of her friend Zuri.

"Zuri was a world traveler who lived to be ninety-two," Great-Grandma explained. "We once talked about the difficulty of finding the ideal mate in life, and this is what Zuri had to say":

When I was young, I wrote a wish list of all the qualities I wanted in my sweetheart, such as humor, intelligence, wisdom, and compassion, and I also wrote out the interests I wanted us to share, such as dancing, traveling, cooking, and so on. First I looked in Paris, where I met Jean, a wonderful soul indeed. Jean matched most of my wish list but wasn't funny and didn't like to dance.

Years later I met Chris in Chicago, who also matched most of my wish list but, to my disappointment, I discovered that Chris wasn't very smart and didn't like to travel. Finally, I met Hoshi in Tokyo, who exactly matched everything on my wish list.

Unfortunately for me, Hoshi also had a wish list.

The wisdom I took from Zuri's story is that if we are looking for someone to perfectly match our wish list, we can expect to be single for a long while, perhaps forever. Perfection is a fantasy. More often than not, the lists of perfect qualities we seek in a mate have less to do with other people's characteristics and more to do with our own insecurities and shortcomings. Until we satisfy within ourselves whatever we perceive to be our own inadequacies, we will never feel satisfied by a relationship.

Despite our best intentions, we tend to attach our sense of self-worth, indeed, our very identity, to external things like relationships, money, appearances, possessions, and prestige. From this skewed perspective, whatever qualities we desire for ourselves but feel we lack, let's say youthfulness, we might try to substitute by creating a relationship with someone whom we perceive as having those qualities. It's an attempt to be youthful by proxy.

This way of filling the gaps that we perceive in ourselves by projecting other people's qualities over our own is illusory. There may be temporary relief, but ultimately there will be further dissatisfaction, as our internal gaps will worsen until we shut the projectors off and start fixing our emotional voids within.

Those of us who tend to project are often looking for mates who can compensate for what we lack. We are looking for a way to feel whole, and we mistakenly believe that the right mate can give that sense of wholeness to us. At the same time, ironically, a person who seems already whole will ultimately be unattractive to us, for if he or she isn't lacking in anything, then what would he or she need us for? Some of us even go so far as to wish that our partners were less successful, or less sexy, or less of something that we are, so that they might depend on us for what they lack. You'd be surprised how many otherwise happy couples break up when one partner acquires, outside the relationship, what he or she had been lacking most.

My friend Diana never had enough money, but her husband always did. For ten years of marriage, he was the major breadwinner, and they were as happy as could be. The minute Diana reversed her situation and began earning more than her husband, however, their marriage started to fall apart. He didn't know his place in the home anymore and was quietly threatened by her success. His identity was so wrapped up in being the provider that he couldn't stay in a relationship with a person who earned more than he did. At first, Diana was confused and hurt by her husband's lack of appreciation for her efforts. She responded with her own anger and selfishness, working longer hours and opening a separate bank account "to spend what I want when I want." Their marriage was spiraling downward until, in a burst of insight, Diana recognized her husband's suffering and her part in contributing to it. By acknowledging her own negativity, Diana empowered herself to make a change in attitude. That opened the door to her husband's realization that his own self-image had been foolishly limited to his role as a breadwinner. They not only saved their relationship, they strengthened it as a result.

*B*eing deeply loved summons your strength;
loving deeply summons your courage.

— LAO-TZU

*L*et your boundless compassion and love
pervade the whole world.

— SUTTA NIPATA

*T*o love is to suffer. To avoid suffering one must not love.
But then one suffers from not loving. Therefore, to love is to suffer
and not to love is to suffer. To suffer is to suffer. To be happy is
to love. To be happy, then, is to suffer. But suffering makes
one unhappy. Therefore, to be unhappy one must love,
or love to suffer, or suffer from too much happiness.
I hope you're getting this down.

— WOODY ALLEN

Buddhist teachers encourage us that the way to achieve absolute happiness in love, as in life, is to take charge of our consciousness and purify our spiritual state of being through continual self-reflection and self-reformation. And there is perhaps no greater means than close loving relationships to help us reveal, and therefore transform, what Buddhism calls the three spiritual poisons of selfishness, anger, and foolishness in our lives.

The Buddhist view of love is a liberating one—it not only recognizes negative forces in relationships, it also teaches that through self-mastery we can perceive the negativity clearly, take responsibility for our share of it, and then fundamentally transform it.

Buddhism teaches that without continual self-reflection and improvement, one of the most surprising discoveries we will find in love is that feelings of rapture can morph into very different feelings—even hate—without a moment's notice. Perhaps even worse than hate is the potential for romantic love to descend into apathy, a state of nonfeeling in which we no longer care enough either to love or to hate. For that very reason, early Buddhist teachings describe romantic love as a lesser type of love—weak, illusionary, and unstable—while compassionate love is seen as a greater type of love—strong, impartial, and limitless.

These two types of love described by early Buddhist scriptures—greater love and lesser love—are also known as compassionate love and needy love. Romantic love was seen as a type of needy love, as were sexual love, affectionate love, and egoistic love. Needy love describes a hungry desire not only for other people but also for material possessions, status, and so on. In needy love, we desire not particular men or women, who are real, but the possession of them, which is an illusion. We are not pleased to simply be with them; we are pleased by the accomplishment of being with them.

Since needy love is based on the narcissism of ego attachment rather than the altruism of compassion, it always carries the potential to change into hate or other negative emotions. In other words, when love based on selfish attachments becomes unfulfilling, this failure on the part of a mate to satisfy one's needs is seen as a betrayal of one's ego. Previously loving emotions toward one's mate can then transform from self-serving romance to self-preserving animosity.

As all forms of needy love were seen to be riddled with this kind of selfishness, anger, and foolishness, early Buddhist teachings viewed needy types of love as deluded, impulsive, and destructive states of life to be avoided.

Later Buddhist teachings placed less emphasis on denying needy forms of love and instead encouraged lovers to redirect their energies to broader, more benevolent, friendship-based forms of love. Lovers would then be free to create with each other a more solid, lasting, and positive relationship based on the realm of compassionate love, seen in Buddhism as the most enlightened foundation for any close relationship.

The ancient Buddhist term for enlightened, compassionate love, *jihi*, combines two words meaning "to sigh" and "friendship." This designation indicates that the heart of true love, or unconditional compassion, is based on friendship that permeates both good times and bad—a willingness to share with our loved ones the laughter of joy and the sighs of pain. "To sigh in friendship" is considered the ultimate expression of love from the Buddhist perspective.

A lifetime without love is like a year without springtime.

— ASIAN PROVERB

*W*hoever has loved knows all that life contains
of sorrow and joy.

— GEORGE SAND

*L*ove has the power to make you believe what you would
normally treat with the deepest suspicion.

— MIRABEAU

*O*ne is very crazy when in love.

— SIGMUND FREUD

No matter how friendly or compassionate we try to be, however, the reality of two lovers attempting to mesh their lives can be messy. Old behavior patterns emerge, personalities clash, emotions run amok, even sex can become, well, problematic. Families interfere, money issues interfere, and even religion can interfere. You name it, it could happen. But how is it that two people in love can come to feel animosity, hatred, or even worse—apathy—toward each other?

According to Buddhism, it is because when we commit ourselves to a life of intimacy with someone, the three spiritual poisons of selfishness, anger, and foolishness are pulled to the surface of our lives. In a kind of spiritual detoxification, the murkiest, unhappiest, least attractive aspects of our character inexplicably emerge through the course of our intimate relationships.

The Buddhist view of love isn't pessimistic, it's realistic. It's common sense. Anyone who has been in a romantic relationship knows that no one can push our buttons the way our sweetheart can. We can hear something from a stranger and think nothing of it, but when the same thing comes from that special someone, our beloved partner, our so-called better half, oh no, watch out. Old wounds open up, and before we know it we are feeling overwhelmed by negative forces—we can't seem to talk without arguing, or trust crumbles between us, or perhaps we have moments of temporary insanity. You know what I'm talking about.

Whatever challenges we face, though, here's the good news: Happiness in love is within our reach.

Putting into practice the advice of Buddhism won't guarantee that a relationship will thrive, let alone survive, but it does provide a tool of empowerment, a path of hope, a way to come out the other side of the tunnel with a stronger relationship or, at the very least, a stronger sense of self. Building happiness in love requires work but, fortunately, as with any noble work, the rewards are sweeter than we can imagine.

Sometimes, after we've witnessed spiritual poisons manifest, our tendency is to withdraw from our mate, either emotionally or literally. In some cases (such as abusive relationships), separating may be the wisest choice, although it is often not a new partner but a new perception that will bring us the fulfillment we seek. When poisons surface in our relationships, we have a choice: We can see them as barriers threatening our relationship or as vital opportunities for growth. It is up to us to decide whether the dark parts within ourselves and our mate will either stop our love or strengthen our love.

A loving relationship is meant to serve not as a safe harbor for our unhealthy tendencies but rather as a healthy place of reformation where such tendencies can be eliminated. Only by exposing the dark spiritual poisons within us can we transform them in the light of spiritual healing.

In this evolutionary (and revolutionary) process of the heart, Buddhism emphasizes that everyone must take responsibility for his or her own happiness. We are not responsible for our sweetheart's behavior or level of happiness (or anyone else's), only for our own. This simple understanding opens our lives to boundless creativity, freedom, and joy. It means that we control every aspect of our love and life—we have the power here and now to improve our relationships in any way we wish by first improving ourselves. Indeed, that is the very goal of Buddhist teachings, to create absolute and unshakable happiness within each individual's life, with or without a significant other. The important point is this: The most fundamental love relationship we can have is with ourselves.

To love oneself is the beginning of a lifelong romance.

—OSCAR WILDE

If you sacrifice your growth and talent for love,
you will not find happiness. True happiness is obtained only
by fully realizing your potential. Love should be a force
that helps you expand your life and bring forth your
innate potential with fresh and dynamic vitality.

—DAISAKU IKEDA

We do not attract that which we want;
we attract that which we are.

—JAMES ALLEN

PART TWO

LOVE AND REALITY

The Inner Path:

FINDING TRUE LOVE WITHIN

Being in love is not finding a perfect person,
but finding an imperfect person perfect.

— ASIAN PROVERB

❦

Love is eternity. It wipes out all sense of time, vanquishing
all memory of a beginning and all fear of an end.

— MADAME DE STAËL

❦

Age cannot protect us from love,
but love can protect us from age.

— JEANNE MOREAU

❦

One who knows one's own heart
knows the equivalent of every wise saying.

— BUDDHIST PROVERB

I've gained many insights from Buddhism about love, but perhaps the most basic is that all of my relationships have one thing in common—me. My condition affects all of my relationships more than anything.

"It is no use to blame the mirror if your face is awry" goes the Buddhist saying. Likewise, the condition of our relationships is a reflection of ourselves, of the karma that we have developed through our thoughts, words, and deeds.

An ancient Japanese comedic tale exemplifies this idea:

> Once, there was a remote country town where no one owned a mirror. The ruling samurai of the area, returning from his visit to the capital, presented his sweetheart with a mirror as a souvenir. Since his beloved had never before seen a mirror, the reflection in it looked like a stranger. Thus began a long fight between them over who the stranger was that the samurai had brought back with him.

Although we can choose to see this as just an amusing story, we can also see it as an illustration of how we can become anguished over events that are nothing but reflections of ourselves. Love relationships in particular can function as a kind of mirror for our lives. When we make a habit of showing respect and compassion for our mate, we will naturally see respect and compassion returned to us. In Buddhism, this principle is called "the oneness of person and environment." As the Buddhist philosopher Nichiren wrote: "When we bow in reverence to other people, the Buddha nature inherent in their lives bows back to us. This is the same as how, when one bows facing a mirror, the reflected image bows back."

Like bowing before a mirror, the images we see in our relationships will precisely align themselves with our own condition.

This is a beautiful and important concept, and it may be one of the most challenging lessons to learn. It is difficult to accept the reality that we hold the key to our wishes within ourselves. But that is exactly the message of Buddhism—that the key to creating indestructible happiness in love, as in life, is found only within ourselves, in the development of our own potential, regardless of external and unreliable factors like relationships.

A loving relationship may provide companionship, a fulfilling sex life, a family, and other basic joys of human existence. But to base one's happiness on it is to fail to see the essential instability of the situation. After all, a lifelong companion will eventually die, and even the greatest sexual relationship can suffer if other factors change.

It is only with the heart that one can see rightly;
what is essential is invisible to the eye.

— ANTOINE DE SAINT-EXUPÉRY

Hatreds never cease by hate, but by love alone;
this is an eternal truth.

— SHAKYAMUNI

*K*indness in words creates confidence.
Kindness in thinking creates profoundness.
Kindness in giving creates love.

— L A O - T Z U

*P*eople change and then forget to tell each other.

— L I L L I A N   H E L L M A N

That powerful word, *change,* is one of the biggest challenges for any relationship. We often resist change within ourselves yet try our best to change our partners. Buddhism teaches that there is nothing we can say or do to change another person. People will change only when they are ready. The only people we have the power to change are ourselves.

The most effective way to move the hearts of others and thereby affect real and lasting change in their behavior is by exercising self-control and becoming happy within ourselves, regardless of what other people do or don't do.

Buddhism explains that when we think of ourselves as separate from our environment, we try to fix or control things outside ourselves, which drains our strength and neutralizes our innate wisdom. But when we see ourselves as deeply connected to everyone and everything around us, when we strive to change our circumstances by first changing ourselves, then we manifest our greatest wisdom and power.

As long as we attempt to change the behavior of anyone other than ourselves, frustration will be the only sure outcome. Trying to improve a relationship by changing your mate's behavior is like trying to improve a roadway by changing your car's tires. It may seem less bumpy for a while, but the potholes will only get bigger until you forget about the car and fix the pavement. In other words, if you want a smoother ride down the road of love, start working on yourself and everything else will improve as well.

As we self-reflect and work to improve and strengthen ourselves, we come to see ourselves more clearly. We see that the myriad relationships in our lives, from the most casual to the deepest bonds, all reflect some piece of our inner selves. As we perceive ourselves more honestly, and as we come to accept both our weaknesses and our strengths, the revelation that each of our relationships reflects back to us hidden aspects of ourselves can be quite surprising, even shocking or dismaying—until we remember that this awareness empowers us to create the life and relationships we desire most.

Are you sitting down? Are you ready to hear this? You—yes, you—are worthy of all the love and joy in the world. Realizing this truth is the first step in building a strong sense of self and thus healthy and satisfying relationships. The next step is taking action through your choices each day, here and now. You have the power to do something about your unsatisfactory relationships and to further improve your healthy ones. Whatever the state of your romantic life, you can look forward to steady, long-term progress by working on yourself first, from the inside out.

*L*ove opens the doors into everything, including and
perhaps most of all, the door into one's own secret,
and often frightening, real self.

— MAY SARTON

❧

*T*rue love is as deep as the ocean.

— ASIAN PROVERB

❧

*R*eal love is not two people clinging to each other;
it can be fostered only between two strong people secure
in their individuality. A shallow person will have only
shallow relationships. If you want to experience real love,
it is important to first sincerely develop a strong self-identity.

— DAISAKU IKEDA

My favorite Buddhist teacher, Daisaku Ikeda, once told me that there are three types of love relationships: dependent, independent, and contributive.

The least happy but most common type of love relationship is dependent, which we often hear about in the West as codependent. In dependent unions, partners give love, but with strings attached. Dependent love is controlling, manipulative, and ultimately selfish.

Think about this: Every choice we make, every action we take, comes down to one criterion—it's what we believe we must do in order to be happy. The more deluded we are, the more our choices reflect that delusion. In dependent love, for example, we may believe "If I keep the house cleaner, my mate will stay home more," or "If I just keep my mouth shut, we won't argue," or "If I try to anticipate my husband's wishes, he will need me more." And so we may believe we are making sacrifices for our loved ones. But if our choices have strings attached to them, they're not as loving or giving as we think.

A happier but less common type of relationship is the independent sort, characterized by mutual respect and a strong sense of individuality. In independent unions, partners give love freely and without expectation. You both do what you do because it is the right thing to do, and not because it will elicit some response from your mate.

The happiest and least common type of love relationship is contributive—an independent relationship in which the partners also share a sense of mission in life. In contributive unions, love is given freely not only for each other's nourishment but also toward the greater good of humanity. Contributive partners are not content to help only themselves but passionately support others to improve their lives and become happy as well. In such relationships, the whole is greater than the sum of its parts.

The widespread incidence of dependent love is one of the greatest causes of unhappiness in modern love relationships. Simply put, dependent love originates in unhappy or otherwise dysfunctional families—stressful home environments in which children meet the needs of adults—as opposed to functional families, in which adults meet the needs of children. In a dysfunctional home, a child must focus his or her emotional, mental, and often physical energy on an adult to achieve or maintain relative feelings of stability. This necessity plants the seeds of controlling and manipulative behavior within the child's personality while taking his or her focus away from personal needs and feelings. When children who have grown up in such an environment reach adulthood, they are likely to seek love relationships as the basis of their personalities, becoming dependent upon others for their sense of identity and security.

Although many of us grew up in families that met most of our needs, or at least some of them, we can all relate to the anguish of unmet childhood expectations. These unmet needs follow us into our adult relationships, aching to be fulfilled, often in the form of dependent love. For those who have grown up in dysfunctional environments, love means being taken care of or, in some cases, taking care of others. When such relationships fail to satisfy their desires, dependent people often turn on their partners in resentment. Those of us who may have developed dependent characteristics must learn to discern the difference between compassion and caretaking, between receiving love and relying on others for happiness, and between helping and manipulating.

*L*ove one another, but make not a bond of love; let it rather be a moving sea between the shores of your souls.

— Kahlil Gibran

❧

*C*ompassionate love is an awakening of the heart from animalistic self-interest to humanity.

— Joseph Campbell

❧

*L*ove is patient; love is kind; love is not envious or boastful or arrogant or rude. It does not insist on its own way; it is not irritable or resentful; it does not rejoice in wrongdoing, but rejoices in truth. It bears all things, believes all things, hopes all things, endures all things.

— I Corinthians 13:4–7

So what are we looking for in a partner? Why do we want a relationship in the first place? Perhaps we seek companionship, security, and a monogamous sexual relationship. Maybe we wish for someone who shares our sense of humor, has a strong character, appreciates the little things in life, and has many other qualities we have not found in one person before. We may wish to meet a "soul mate," but once we find him or her, then what? Do we expect simply to live happily ever after? Are the long lists of characteristics we seek in a companion our true desires or merely illusions containing deeper, hidden motivations?

Maybe we feel profoundly lonely or feel the need to be loved because we are unsure of our self-worth. Perhaps we are driven by restless sexual desire or are trapped in patterns of unhealthy relationships rooted in childhood trauma. Whatever the case, the common denominator of these and countless other motives is that we tend to rely upon something other than our own inherent wisdom—our Buddha nature, which we all have—to build feelings of security and satisfaction.

Are we seeking someone with whom we can share our lives and work toward our dreams, or are we looking for someone to fill a void in our lives?

Everyone wants to feel a sense of wholeness, of connectedness. This longing for communion is at the very root of our desire to love and be loved, to feel at one with others and thereby be reassured of our wholeness. Buddhism teaches, however, that all of our suffering in love (and in life) ultimately arises from looking outside ourselves for happiness. Today, perhaps more than ever, people have been deluded into believing that the key to their happiness lies in the reformation of their external world—their appearance, their home, their mate, and so on. Buddhism teaches that nothing could be further from the truth, and that to seek one's salvation externally is to chase an illusion, ultimately causing great suffering. No one can truly make us feel complete, or happy, or anything else. With or without a partner, we are solely responsible for the state of our emotions.

*W*e don't love what we desire,
we desire what we love.

— SHAKYAMUNI

✧

*T*he whole difference between construction and
creation is exactly this: that a thing constructed can
only be loved after it is constructed; but a thing created
is loved before it exists.

— CHARLES DICKENS

✧

*L*ove is pleasure accompanied by the idea
of an external cause, just as hatred is pain
accompanied by the idea of an external cause.

— BARUCH SPINOZA

One of the most helpful spiritual lessons I've ever learned came to me from Mrs. Jay, a wise old Buddhist who lived in my neighborhood while I was growing up. Whenever I would help Mrs. Jay carry her groceries home, she would reward me with a handful of candies and an earful of wisdom.

On one such occasion, when I was about eleven years old, Mrs. Jay explained to me that we are each individually responsible for our circumstances and for our own emotional, mental, and physical well-being. No one else can truly make us happy or make us feel anything we don't wish to feel. She taught me that the common statements "You make me happy when you do this" and "You make me angry when you do that" are based on the illusion that other people have power over our emotions. If that were the case, then their behavior would have to change before we could feel any different. But that is false.

Mrs. Jay encouraged me to recognize that in any given situation I am the only one who can decide what I will feel—anger, happiness, or any other emotion. She taught me, from that point on, to use the more accurate phrasing "When you do that, I feel . . . "

Years later, my grandmother built upon this teaching by sharing with me the following advice from her mentor, Josei Toda, of the Soka Gakkai Buddhist association. Mr. Toda said:

When we are upset, it's easy to blame others. The true cause of our feelings, however, is within us. For example, imagine yourself as a glass of water. Now, imagine past negative experiences as sediment at the bottom of your glass. Next, think of an unpleasant situation as a spoon. When the spoon stirs, the sediment clouds your water. It may appear that the spoon caused the water to cloud—but if there were no sediment, the water would remain clear. Even if we remove the spoon, our sediment still remains— lying in wait for the next spoon to appear. On the other hand, if we remove our sediment, then no matter how a spoon may stir, our water will remain clear.

By weaving this understanding into the fabric of our lives, we can begin to rectify any source of unhappiness at its most fundamental level. We will see that our inner transformation has the unfathomable power to help ourselves and others in ways that no other actions or words ever could. We will come to understand that we must take care of our own needs and feelings ourselves, while being mindful not to use or abuse others in the process. It may take time and effort but, in the end, we will prove to ourselves that no strategy is as powerful as one based on self-mastery.

As we continue to remove the sediment from our lives and develop our enlightened potential, our life condition naturally rises. This is extremely important, since Buddhism teaches that we tend to attract people who share our predominant life condition, whether we outwardly exhibit similar characteristics of that state or not.

According to the Buddhist concept of the Ten Worlds, we can envision our life condition—our "world," so to speak, or basic tendency in our daily lives and relationships—as part of a pyramid. At any given moment, our life condition resides in one step of this pyramid. The broad base of the pyramid represents the life condition of Buddhahood, or ultimate wisdom, with the progressively narrower levels representing the other nine worlds. The top corner of the pyramid represents the state of Hell, or ultimate delusion. If our predominant life condition were that of Hell, our relationships would balance precariously on its sharp tip. Anything could shake them up or knock them down. The more expansive the foundation of our life condition, the better our chances at forging stable, contributive relationships.

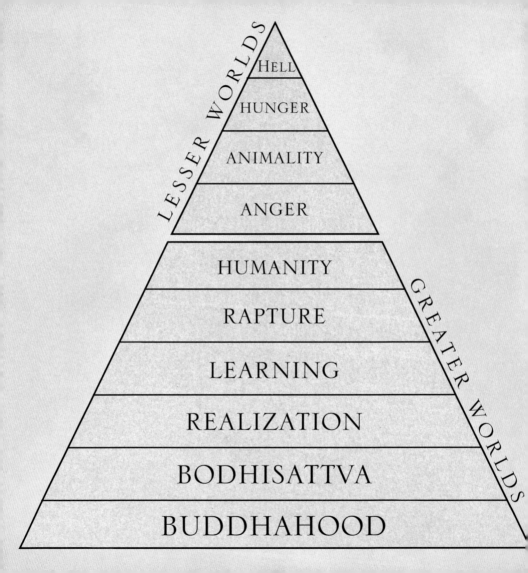

The Buddhist concept of the Ten Worlds illustrates the changing conditions of life that human beings experience from day to day. While a person can experience any or all of these conditions on a daily basis, a single life condition tends to dominate.

LESSER WORLDS

HELL (ULTIMATE DELUSION)
Hopeless, destructive, overwhelming suffering.
The world of Hell is a condition in which everything becomes a source of misery.

HUNGER
Fixation by insatiable desires.
The world of Hunger is governed by endless desire for profit, power, pleasure, and so on.

ANIMALITY
Bullying of the weak, ingratiating of the strong.
The world of Animality is controlled by base instincts, exhibiting a fear of the strong and a despisement of the weak.

ANGER
Arrogant, ego-driven behavior.
The world of Anger is dominated by ego and arrogance and is characterized by animosity and persistent, if not overt, aggressiveness.

GREATER WORLDS

HUMANITY
Reasonable, logical behavior.
The world of Humanity is a tranquil state in which one tries to control desires and impulses and act in harmony with others.

RAPTURE
Intense elation from fulfilled desires.
The world of Rapture is a blissful condition of temporary elation from the fulfillment of some desire.

LEARNING
Seeking happiness through others' teachings.
The world of Learning is an awakening to the impermanence of all things through the teachings of others.

REALIZATION
Seeking happiness through direct experience.
*The world of Realization holds deep understanding of the impermanence
of all things, seeking truth through self-reflection and reformation.*

BODHISATTVA (COMPASSION)
Devotion to the happiness of others.
*The world of Bodhisattva is characterized by loving-kindness,
seeking happiness by working for the well-being of others.*

BUDDHAHOOD (ULTIMATE WISDOM)
Enlightened, altruistic, unshakable happiness.
*The world of Buddhahood is a state of absolute freedom in which
one recognizes the true nature of life and the universe.*

In the lesser worlds, *I love you* means "I desire you, I want to obtain something from your existence." In the greater worlds, *I love you* means "I treasure you, I want to contribute to your existence." Love dominated by life conditions of the lesser worlds is based on the ego, and in such states, we welcome others' love as a reflection of our own self-idolization, a kind of emotional moonlight mistaken for the light of the sun. What we really need are rays of self-love, based on the sunshine of the greater life conditions, particularly that of Buddhahood.

From the Buddhist perspective, self-love is crucial, yet self-love based on the lesser worlds is arrogant and conceited, strongly unattractive to others no matter how beautiful our exterior facade may seem. In contrast, self-love based on the greater worlds is strongly attractive to others, no matter how ordinary the details of our life may be. Self-love based on the greater worlds is not egoism but a wise person being a loving friend to himself or herself.

One of the best things you can do for your love life is to first fall in love with yourself. You know how people say that when someone is in love she or he is so very attractive? Imagine how attractive you'd be if you could be in love all the time. You *can*—with yourself.

"Why love myself?" you may ask. "What is lovable about me?" If you don't have answers, you can start working on them today. Before you know it, someone else will be telling you why you are so lovable, too.

Enlightenment is another word for loving yourself, completely and unconditionally, imperfections and all. Trying to be someone you are not for the sake of someone else's love (or for any reason) is a sure way to suffer. People don't want to love the fake you— they want to love the real you. Despite what you may think, your idiosyncrasies are even more endearing to others than your greatest triumphs. Relax. Be yourself. You are who you are for a purpose, and you will only discover that purpose by living true to yourself.

When you truly love who you are, you will be truly loved for who you are. When you continually grow and advance, little by little, living true to yourself each moment, you will feel a flowing sense of joy and have confidence that tomorrow can always be better than today.

If you are unsatisfied with the choices you've made in your past or present relationships, you can reflect upon them and identify which of the Ten Worlds have dominated them. You may find remarkable similarities in negative patterns of communication and behavior both in yourself and in others. This is what Buddhism calls your negative karma, or destructive patterns of behavior you may feel compelled to repeat. It is to break free from such patterns that Buddhism urges the daily practice of self-reflection and self-reformation.

Through the process of self-mastery, you will naturally come to view your past and present relationships in a different light—the light of wisdom. From the Buddhist view, the ideal foundation for any close relationship is wisdom, characterized by a deep spiritual bond and the respect and compassion that naturally develop as we continue to grow and learn. Wisdom in Buddhism is, simply put, the capacity to perceive life wholly and objectively. In the area of love, it is the ability to see ourselves clearly and to stay consciously aware of the intentions we bring to our relationships. All affairs of love ultimately return to one's character as a human being. Those who refuse to own their feelings and actions and instead blame other people tend to be shallow of character, difficult, distant, and arrogant. Those who exercise self-mastery tend to be deep of character and find it easy to show boundless love and compassion toward others. In either case, what we give out we will also receive.

It is better to love than to be loved.

—ARISTOTLE

❧

We don't love others when we find them beautiful,
we find others beautiful when we love them.

—JOSEI TODA

Love does not consist of gazing at each other,
but looking outward together in the same direction.

— ANTOINE DE SAINT-EXUPÉRY

When one chants *Nam-myoho-renge-kyo*
even during sexual union, then earthly desires are enlightenment
and the sufferings of birth and death are nirvana.

— NICHIREN

Buddhism teaches that the more deeply we consider our relationship patterns, the more we may come to see that the same characteristics that originally attracted us to certain people are the very things that eventually repelled us from them. For example, let's say that, through the rose-colored glasses of love, Tyler was charmed by Jamie's easygoing attitude. They started a romance, time passed, and as the rapture faded, Tyler became increasingly irritated by what she then saw as Jamie's procrastination and lack of motivation. In other words, Tyler was both attracted to and repelled from Jamie by the same characteristic. The only difference was in Tyler's changed perception, as her life condition inevitably settled from the temporary ecstasy of Rapture to the more mundane realities of Humanity and beyond.

Like Tyler, we all too often fall in love with people for who they aren't (our projected ideal of perfection) and then leave them for who they are (less than perfect people, just like us).

My father once told me it's like feeling that "the wicked witch has killed the fair maiden," except that the wicked witch and the fair maiden are the same person. The partner you lacked, the woman you dreamed about and desired, was the fair maiden. If you allow your life condition to shrink into the lesser worlds, however, then the fair maiden you married, the one you came to feel you possessed and no longer needed, she became the wicked witch. The difference was less in her and more in your changed perception of her. Likewise, if the fair maiden's life condition narrows, creating a shift in her perspective, then her Prince Charming might just as easily turn into an evil dragon.

When we neglect the practice of self-reflection, our life condition can easily shrink into the lesser worlds and, more than ever, we will seem to notice things in other people that bother us. It's interesting to note, however, that when we take a good look at the traits that irritate us most about other people, we often discover the same traits within ourselves.

The more we deny certain traits of our own, the more we feel threatened or irritated by similar traits in others. My friend Adam was a blatantly homophobic jock who just couldn't stand gay people, that is, until he finally accepted his own sexuality. For the past seven years, Adam's been living happily with his boyfriend, Steve. My former colleague Bailey was convinced that the president of our company was the most oppressive person alive. It turns out that the real problem was not our boss, who was generally kind, but Bailey's hidden control issues. My cousin Robin used to complain compulsively about people who lie—so I suggested that he might need to look within at his own sense of integrity, an eye-opening experience for him.

Equally interesting is that sources of attraction also hold deep clues to our character. We can learn more about ourselves not by whom we are attracted to but by *why* we are attracted to them. When we feel attracted to someone, we should try to perceive the nature of our attraction *before* we become involved. Our karma to be attracted to certain types of people may be strong, and if our Buddha nature, our inherent wisdom, warns against involvement, then we must either heed the warning or face the consequences.

In this context, Buddhism encourages the lifelong practice of self-reformation as a means of developing the good fortune to meet the person who is right for us at the right time. If we are already involved with someone, the art of self-reflection can help us develop the wisdom both to recognize the potential that exists in the relationship and to decide how to act accordingly.

For some people, the practice of self-mastery entails prayer, meditation, exercise, writing, or other forms of mental, emotional, or physical focus. My favorite practice is the Buddhist chant *Nam-myoho-renge-kyo,* which has proven to be the most effective means of improvement for my life. Whatever method you choose, the goal is the same—to perceive yourself clearly and to manifest the wisdom, courage, and compassion to create the relationships that you desire most, here and now. You, like me and all of us, have the power to shape your life to reflect your greatest, most enlightened self. What better motivation could there be to cultivate self-mastery and self-love?

If you truly loved yourself, you would never harm another.

— SHAKYAMUNI

*A*bsence is to love what wind is to fire;
it extinguishes the small, it enkindles the great.

— COMTE DE BUSSY-RABUTIN

*N*o one has ever loved anyone
the way everyone wants to be loved.

— MIGNON MCLAUGHLIN

*L*ove is a word used to label the sexuality of the young,
the habituation of the middle-aged,
and the dependency of the old.

— JOHN CIARDI

PART THREE

LOVE AND LIFE

The Middle Path:

CREATING ROMANTIC HAPPINESS NOW

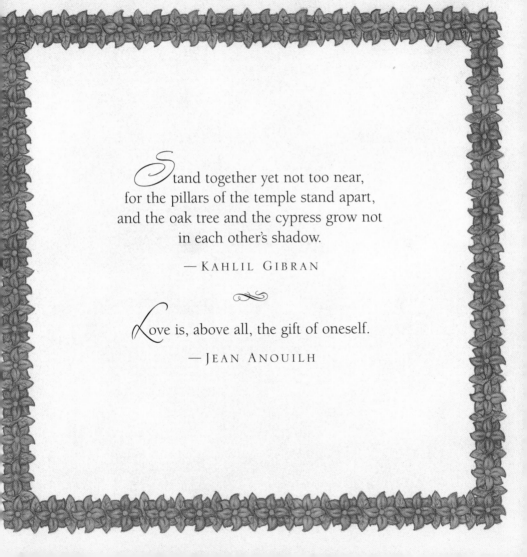

Stand together yet not too near,
for the pillars of the temple stand apart,
and the oak tree and the cypress grow not
in each other's shadow.

— KAHLIL GIBRAN

Love is, above all, the gift of oneself.

— JEAN ANOUILH

I love you not only for who you are,
but for who I am when I am with you.

— ROY CROFT

*O*ne advantage of marriage, it seems to me,
is that when you fall out of love with each other,
it keeps you together until you have a chance
to fall in love again.

— JUDITH VIORST

A favorite Buddhist saying of mine is that in love, as in life, the things we fear most have already happened to us. Your greatest fear in love—losing your freedom or your individuality, being hurt, abandoned, controlled, betrayed, you name it—reveals the pain you have already suffered. There is also comfort in this thought, for you have already faced your worst fear. As long as you retain the wisdom gained from that experience and let go of the pain, then you need not repeat the past.

Unfortunately, your automatic, subconscious reactions to the fear of feeling the same hurt again may cause you to avoid getting too close to people. In that case, no matter how much you desire companionship, you will not find it to your satisfaction. Until you let go of the fear that binds you, you will continue to push away opportunities for happiness in love.

To break the cycle, you must recognize that your emotional defense mechanisms are attracting more pain than they deter. Herein you encounter a dilemma, for while you feel the need to relinquish the defenses that may be harming your relationships, you also feel the need to hold on to them. After all, those ingenious forms of emotional insulation are what helped you get through to this point.

Buddhism encourages us to replace defensive, fear-based

reactions with thoughtful, proactive responses. Reactions tend to be irresponsible and impulsive, whereas responses, as the word itself hints, are *respons*ible and considered. Reactions are based upon fixed beliefs and expectations from prior experiences. Responses are based on the present moment and what that moment requires.

When I was growing up, my mother often said to me, "Fear is an illusion. It is an acronym for False Evidence Appearing Real. When fear is based on past events rather than present-moment awareness, your reactions to it will invariably result in different outcomes than you hoped." Her words have proven true, particularly in the context of love.

If you are holding on to the pain of betrayal, for example, you may experience fear when your current mate even looks at another person. Your partner may be completely faithful, yet you still react with jealousy. Instead of drawing your mate closer to you, such fear-based reactions only serve to push him or her further away.

When you can separate similar behaviors between different people, you are able to respond wisely. Your mate's actions are his or her sole responsibility, but the way you *feel* about your mate's actions is your own responsibility. No one can truly make you feel insecure, unworthy, or inferior—except you.

Nevertheless, subconsciously associating people in your life today with people from your past can be a hard habit to break. In a split second, you analyze subtle behaviors, superficial appearances, and countless other clues, matching them with profiles of people from your past. He reminds you of your father, she reminds you of your mother, and so on. Sometimes your reactions to people are based solely on these associations. When you subconsciously associate people today with others from your past, there is a danger that you will automatically perceive current circumstances not as what they are but as repeat performances of previous experiences.

Each time you sense you are hearing echoes from the past or feel the impulse to react in the same old way, stop and think— think about what is really going on here and now, if it truly is the same as past experiences, and then respond appropriately. When you react in fear, you limit your choices, closing yourself off. When you carefully respond, you expand your options, opening your life to new possibilities.

$\mathcal{T}$here is no love where there is no will.

— MAHATMA GANDHI

$\mathcal{T}$o the world you may be but one person,
But to one person you may be the world.
What a grand thing, to be loved!
What a grander thing still, to love!

— VICTOR HUGO

$\mathcal{H}$appiness is not something that someone else, like a lover,
can give to us. We must achieve it for ourselves by developing
our character and capacity as human beings.

— DAISAKU IKEDA

The Buddhist teaching of karma, or cause and effect, can guide us through the process of breaking our reactive patterns. Our karma is the sum of our past actions, both positive and negative—the balance of which will eventually return to us in kind. According to this concept, our actions in the past have shaped our present reality, and our actions in the present will direct our future. The concept of karma applied to love explains that our thoughts, words, and deeds navigate the course of our relationships. The bottom line is this: You're in charge, and if you're looking for a specific future, you need to take action now to create it.

If you're unhappy with your current relationship, for example, and you would like it to improve, you must take the action, create the karma, for it to improve. Passively wishing for your relationship to improve and taking action for it to improve are very different causes that will create very different effects. Wishes without actions are ineffective at producing change. Wishes brought to life by actions are the catalysts for all real progress.

The most important goal of a love relationship, according to Buddhism, is the spiritual and emotional growth of each partner. Only by taking action to develop oneself—in other words, creating the karma for healthy progress—can each partner contribute to the lasting growth of a relationship.

My friend Jason is a good example of this. He was unhappy with his wife for many years but had resigned himself to suffer in silence. Eventually, he could stand it no more. Balancing on the edge of saying good-bye, he decided to give his relationship one last chance. His wish was to create a more supportive, communicative, and loving partnership.

He had tried doing nothing. He had tried changing his wife. Neither helped. Finally, he determined to focus on the one thing he knew he could change—himself.

This shift in perspective set in motion a deep inner revolution for Jason, inspiring him to take new actions toward his goal. His life condition broadened as a result, and he began to recognize that, above all, he needed to respect and cherish himself first. If he couldn't, then how could he expect his wife to?

As Jason's way of seeing changed, he also gained a deeper sense of appreciation for all the good they shared as a couple. As he opened himself to become a more supportive, communicative, and loving husband, he found that his wife spontaneously followed his lead. By having taken clear and decisive action to improve their relationship, they are happier in love than ever before.

As in Jason's experience, if you and your partner both take action to create a happier, more contributive relationship, your bond will surely strengthen, perhaps beyond your greatest expectations. If your partner is unwilling, however, your actions alone will not salvage the relationship. At the end of the day, a healthy relationship requires a shared vision between two motivated people.

Sometimes, despite how much two people care for each other, they both realize that their dominant desire is to part ways. So it was with me and my college sweetheart. We were content until our senior year of university, when we realized we had been growing apart. Fortunately, we shared our feelings openly with each other—feelings that vacillated between breaking up and staying together. We eventually bade each other a friendly good-bye, and I continue to think of that relationship warmly.

At the time, however, I was a brokenhearted young man and filled far too many pages of my journal with mushy entries about our failed love. After all, breaking up, no matter how right it may be, is never painless. Reading through that journal recently, I discovered that, despite my youthful naïveté, I did manage to reflect and make some sense out of the whole experience. The closing line of that entry, in particular, still strikes a chord. In it, I likened our love affair to a painting created by us, the two artists. "No matter how sincerely the artists wish it," I wrote, "the colors they long to see will not magically appear on the canvas—

they must act together, thoughtfully and with clear intentions, to make the images of their individual dreams into a unified, beautiful reality."

That experience and others since have taught me that, no matter what the outcome of a relationship, the outcome of a commitment to self-reflection and improvement will always be a positive one. Even if your relationship ends, you will have gained through the practice of self-mastery a deeper sense of self-love and compassion—qualities that will surely see you through the sad times while opening up a thousand new possibilities for unimaginable happiness in the future.

$\mathcal{W}$ho travels for love finds a hundred miles
not longer than one.

— JAPANESE PROVERB

$\mathcal{T}$is better to have loved and lost
than never to have loved at all.

— ALFRED, LORD TENNYSON

$\mathcal{W}$ork together with your mate like the sun and
the moon, a pair of eyes, or the two wings of a bird.
With the sun and the moon, how can you fall into the paths
of darkness? With a pair of eyes, how can you fail to see
the faces of all the Buddhas of the universe?
With a pair of wings, you will surely be able to fly
in an instant to the Buddha land of eternal happiness.

— NICHIREN

Throughout this book we've discussed the importance of developing our powers of self-reflection, wisdom, and compassion. But what about the fiery sparks of romance? The heat of passion is often spontaneous, so how are we supposed to do all the contemplation and self-reformation that Buddhism teaches without losing the excitement and fun of the moment? If we are too cautious to give a relationship a try in the first place, then how will we ever know to whom we want to commit ourselves? Even failed relationships can be valuable in the lessons that we learn from them.

Although these are good points, we must ask ourselves— what do we gain from a series of failed, short-term relationships? Do we become more hopeful or more pessimistic? Are we creating actions that will lead us to greater happiness in love, or are we strengthening our unhappy karmic tendencies?

Our current cultural stage of sexual permissiveness would deem it natural, even healthy, for us to have many intimate relationships before we finally settle down with "the right one." In the Buddhist view, the question is not one of morality but one of pragmatism. How many people have benefited from this trend of serial love relationships with longer, stronger commitments?

Of course, the value of a relationship cannot be gauged by its duration alone. But if we are serious about finding "the right one" and having a loyal, lasting bond with that person, we must also realize the importance of first creating the conscious intention to do so. Otherwise, we leave the back gate open for escape in case our needs are not met to our expectations. This is also an important point in light of the principle of karma. Drifting into a relationship halfheartedly is tantamount to making the cause for it to end at the earliest difficulty, with all the inevitable pain that outcome entails.

On the other hand, we may be serious enough to consider marriage, which Buddhism views as a relationship with eternal impact. Since Buddhism teaches that life is eternal, with no absolute beginning or end, then when a couple makes a vow for life, they make a vow forever. Such a meaningful decision is certainly worthy of many weeks, months, or even years of consideration, until we can confidently base our choice upon the calm of our wisdom rather than the waves of our emotional excitement.

This is not to say, of course, that we must view such commitment in love as a multiple life sentence without possibility of parole. We will enjoy much happier love lives if we instead see romantic commitments as an evolving, conscious choice.

I recently attended a Jewish-Buddhist wedding where my aunt Tomee shared an eloquent analogy. From the Buddhist perspective, she said, the people to whom we commit ourselves in love become mirrors to see ourselves more clearly and, likewise, we become mirrors for them to better see themselves. If we don't like the reflection that we see, we are always free to turn away. As long as we commit to reflect upon ourselves together with the one we love, however, we become two mirrors facing each other, opening dual images of eternity.

$\mathcal{I}$ have loved you in numberless forms, numberless times, in life after life, in age after age, forever.

— RABINDRANATH TAGORE

⤺⤻

$\mathcal{A}$ successful relationship requires falling in love many times, always with the same person.

— MIGNON MCLAUGHLIN

$\mathcal{W}$e cannot consider ourselves truly married until we understand every word our spouse is not saying.

— LORD MANCROFT

$\mathcal{W}$hen a couple has shared the joys and sorrows of life over a long period of time, a deep tie grows between them that cannot be severed by outside forces. It is something broad and deep; a sense of shared destiny.

— DAISAKU IKEDA

Have we come any closer to answering our original question? What is this thing called love anyway?

In the Buddhist view, love—in all its forms—has inspired some of the world's greatest works of art and musical masterpieces. But love, when dominated by spiritual poisons, has also inspired senseless destruction and violence. Love can nurture the realization of dreams or hold people in vicious cycles of abuse. Love may be a diversion, a scapegoat, a joy, a nightmare, or an impetus for personal growth.

In any case, love is as unique as the person experiencing it; it is a reflection of one's life. In the light of Buddhism, love is whatever we are; it is whatever we choose to make it. It's completely within our power to determine, for we shape our love as we shape ourselves.

Awakening to this truth is the first step in building a stronger sense of self and thus healthier and more satisfying relationships. Always remembering that we are worthy of all the love and joy in the world, the next step is taking positive action through our choices each day, starting here and now, to create the love and life of our dreams.